Directors & Movies

2nd Collection

If you like this Book and don't have the 1st Collection, go and get it now!

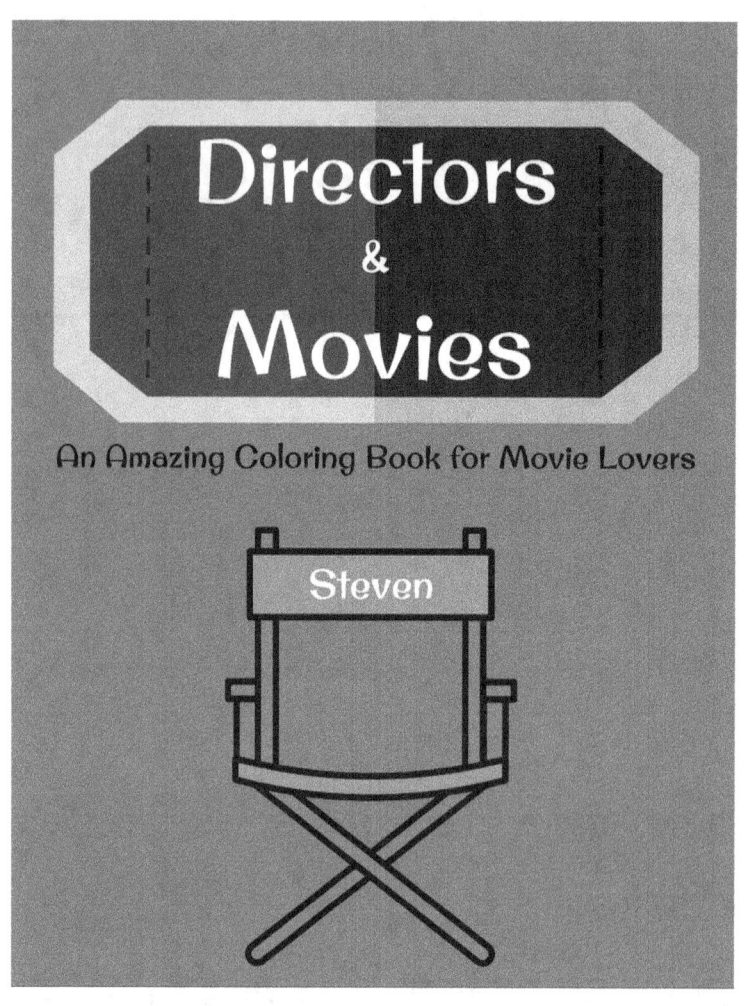

Empty Back

TO BE ABLE TO TAKE THE PAGES OUT OF THE BOOK AND USE IT ANY OTHER WAY!

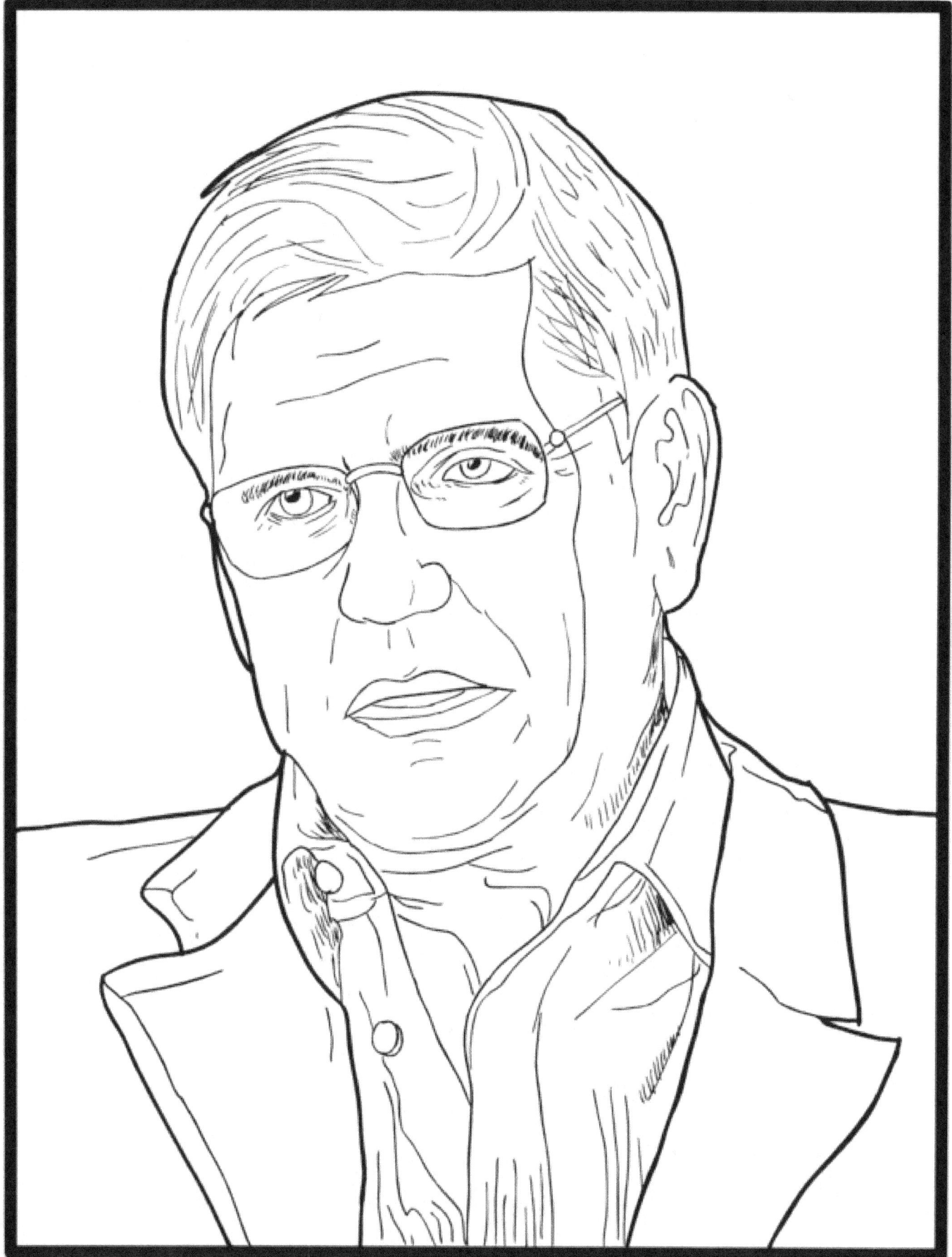

DIRECTOR
ROBERT ZEMECKIS

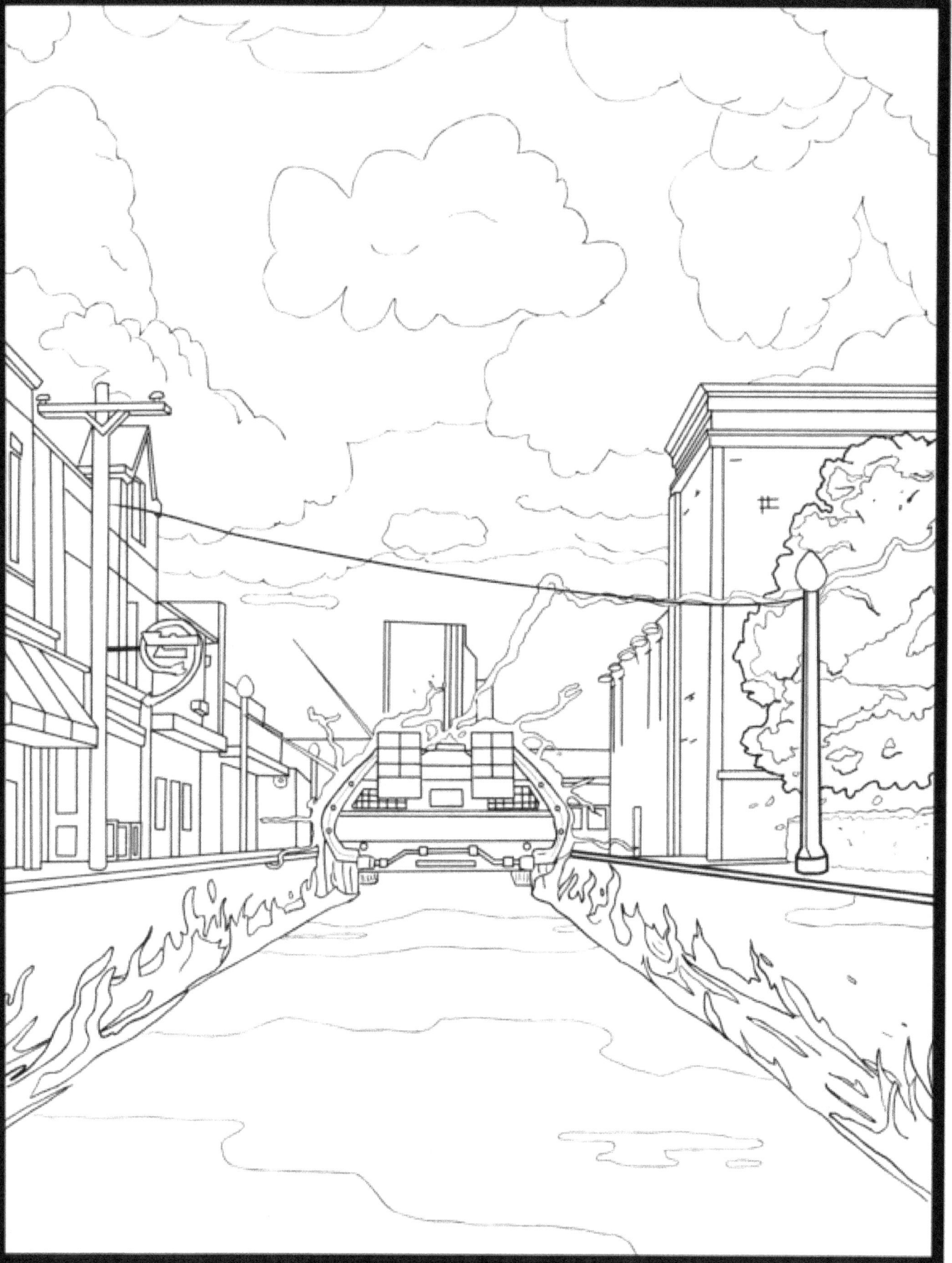

(1985)
BACK TO
THE FUTURE

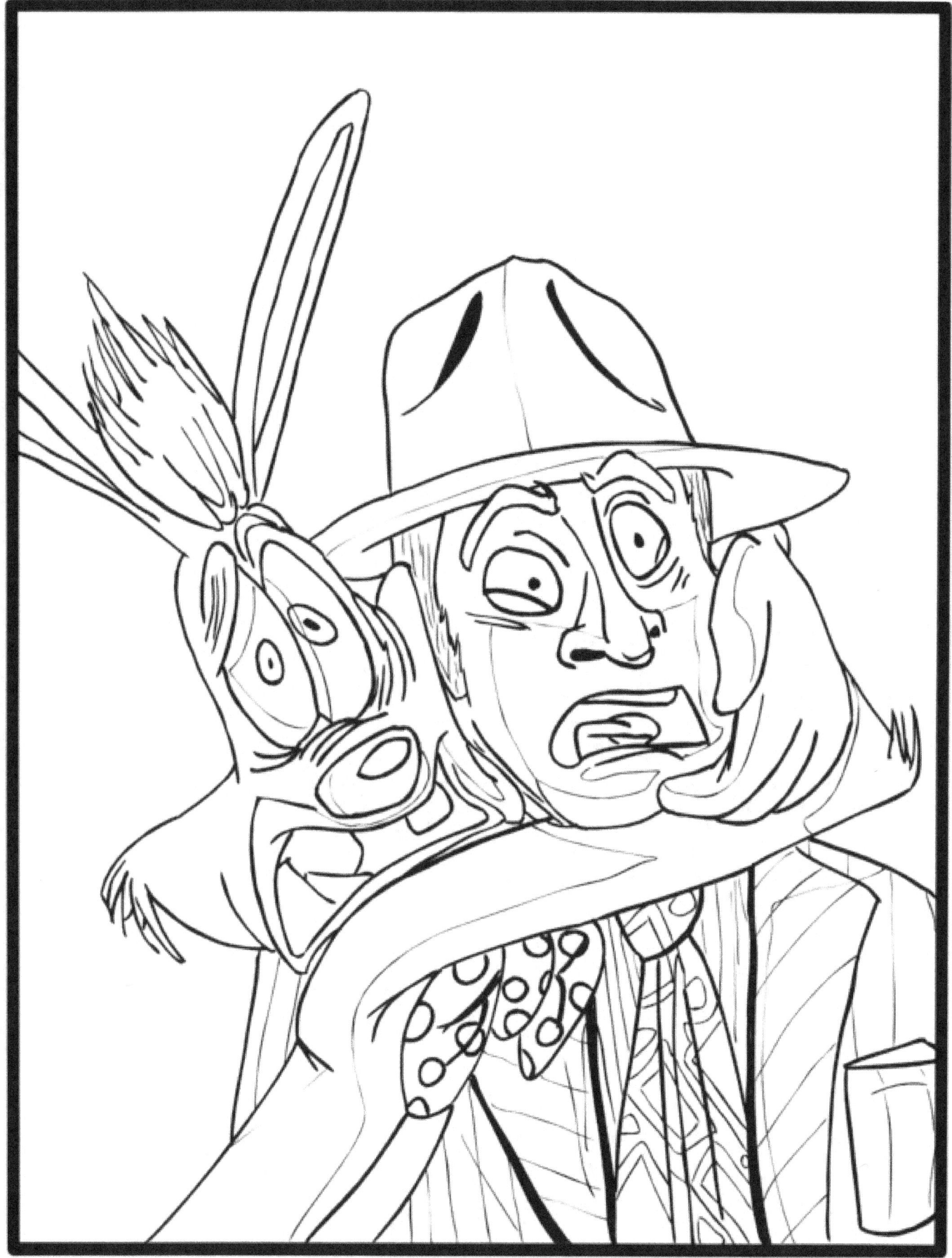

(1988)
WHO FRAMED ROGER RABBIT

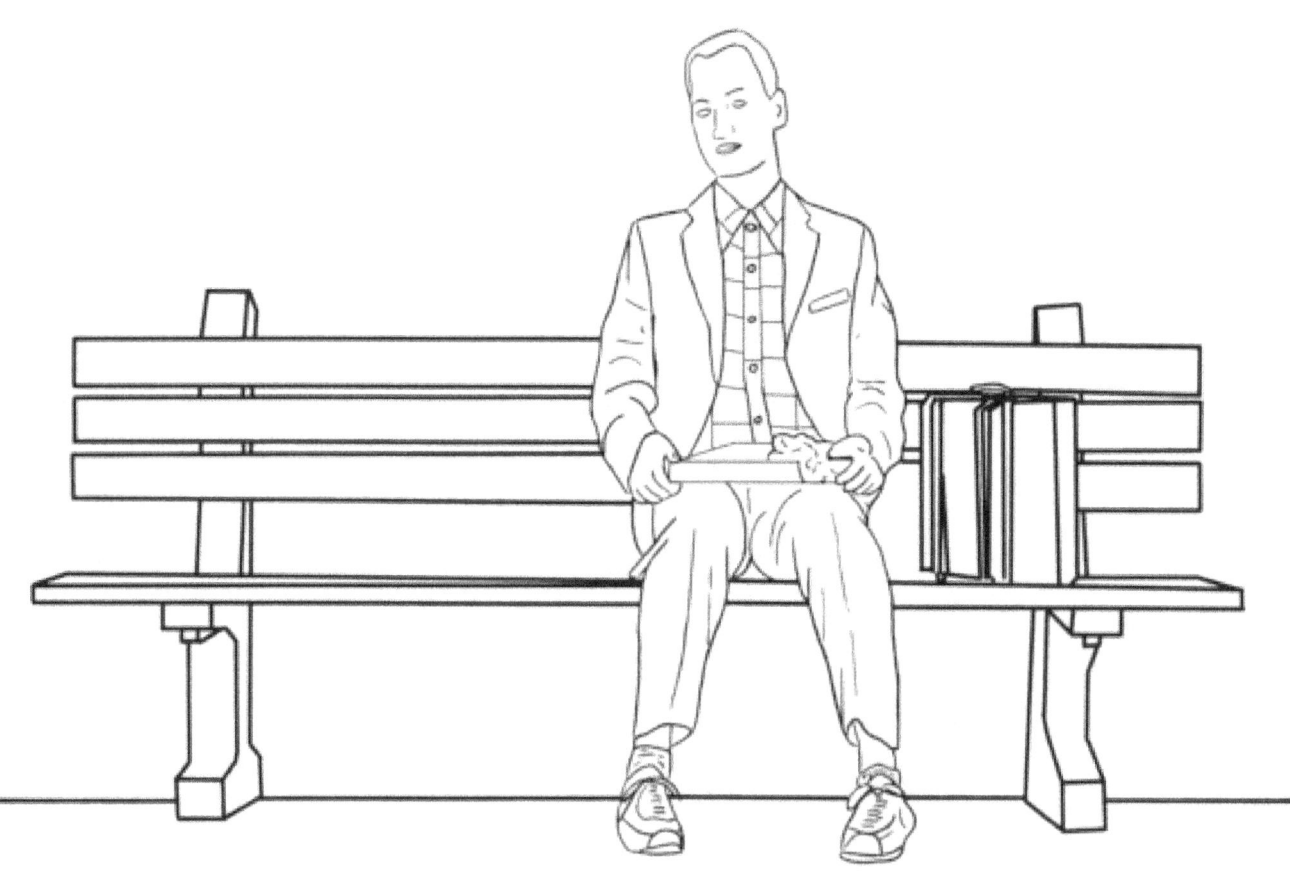

(1994)
FORREST GUMP

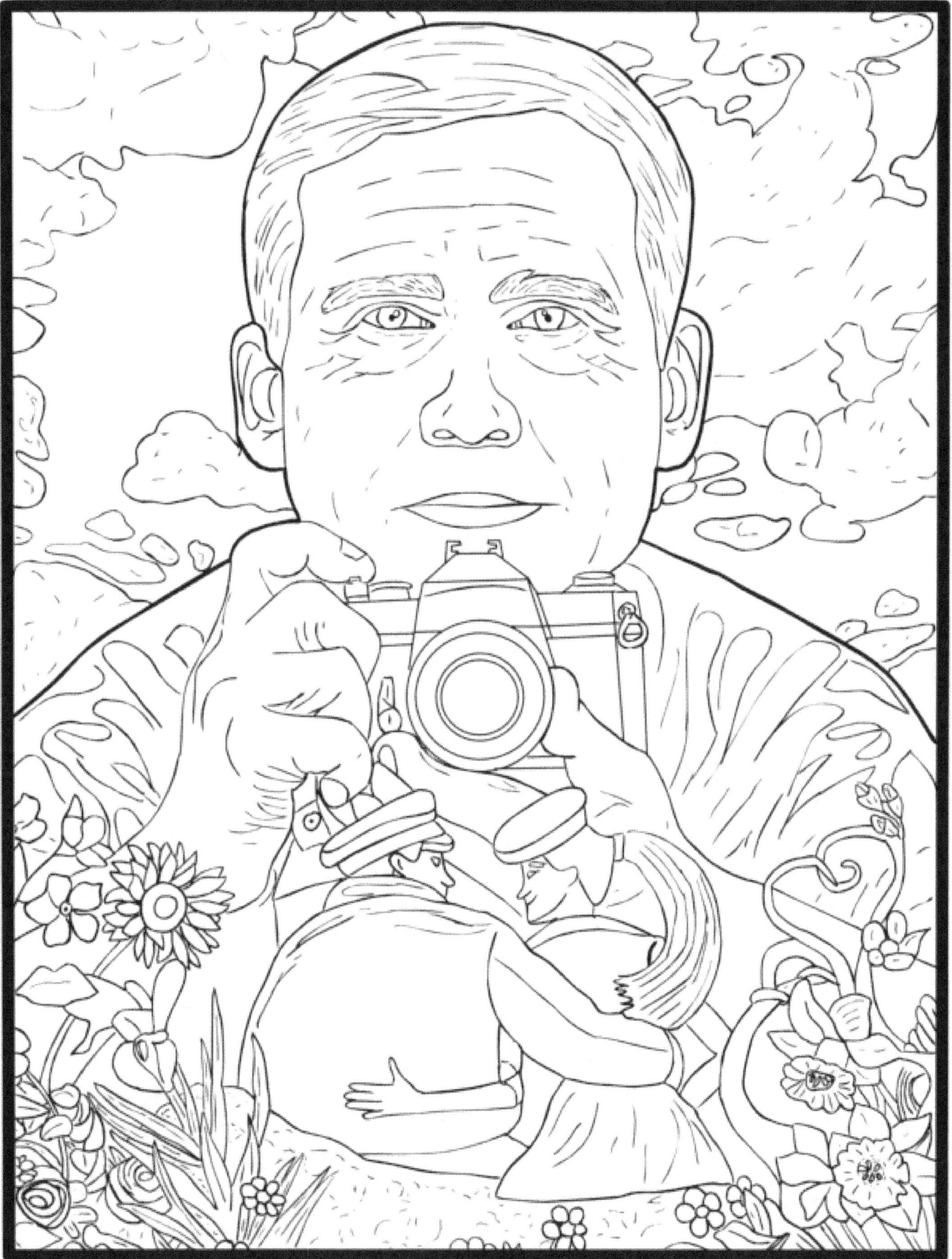

(2018) WELCOME TO MARWEN

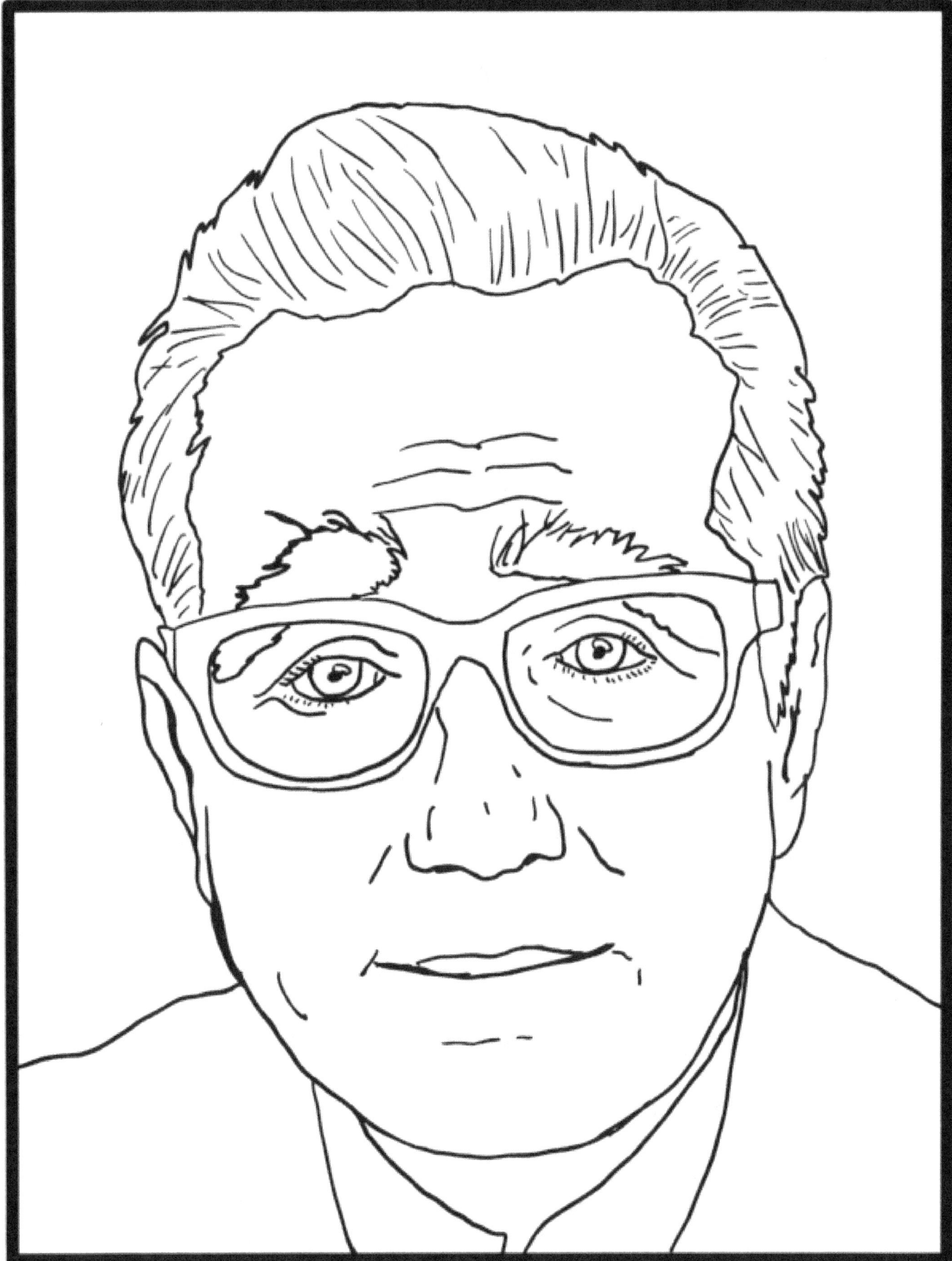

DIRECTOR
MARTIN SCORSESE

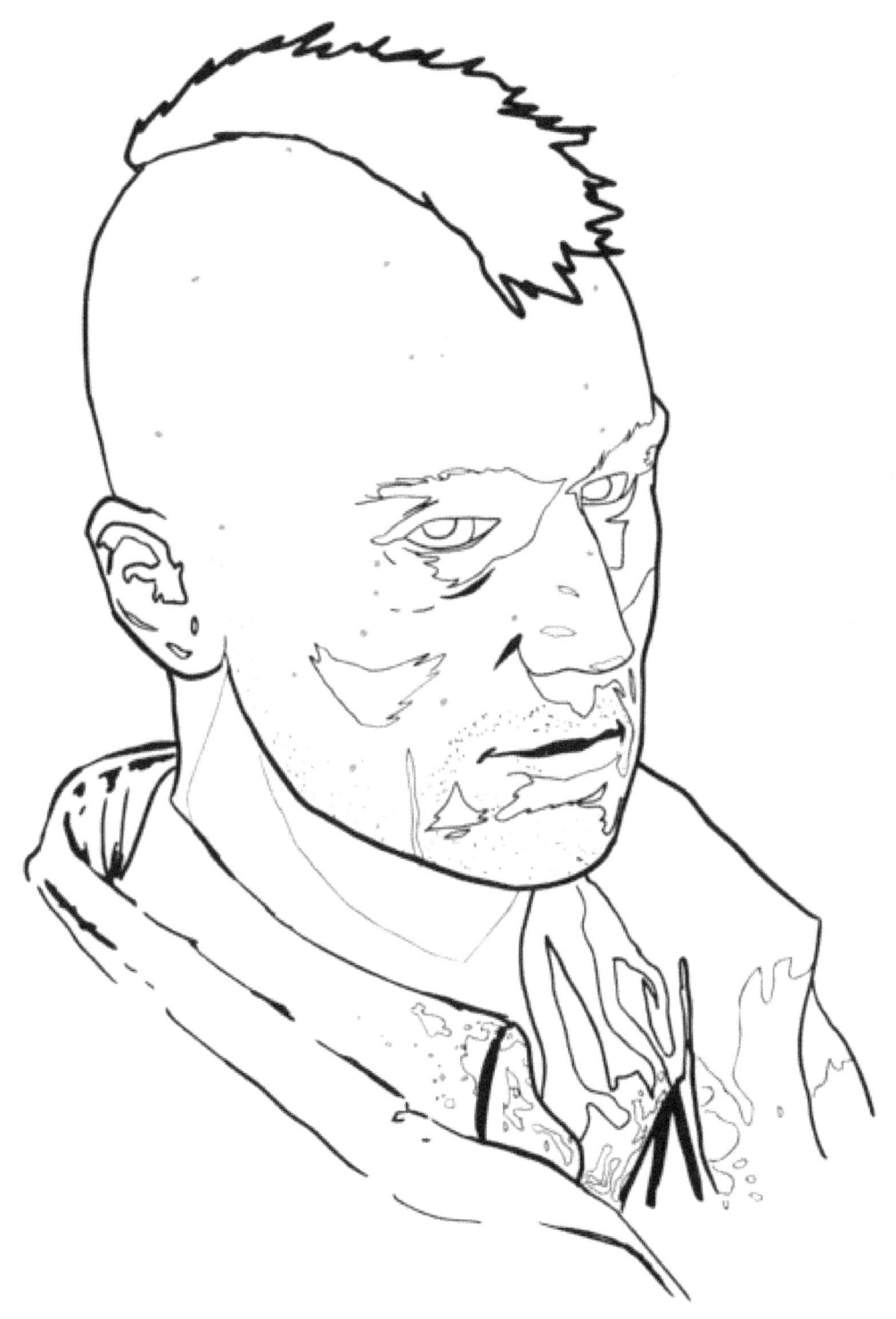

(1976)
TAXI DRIVER

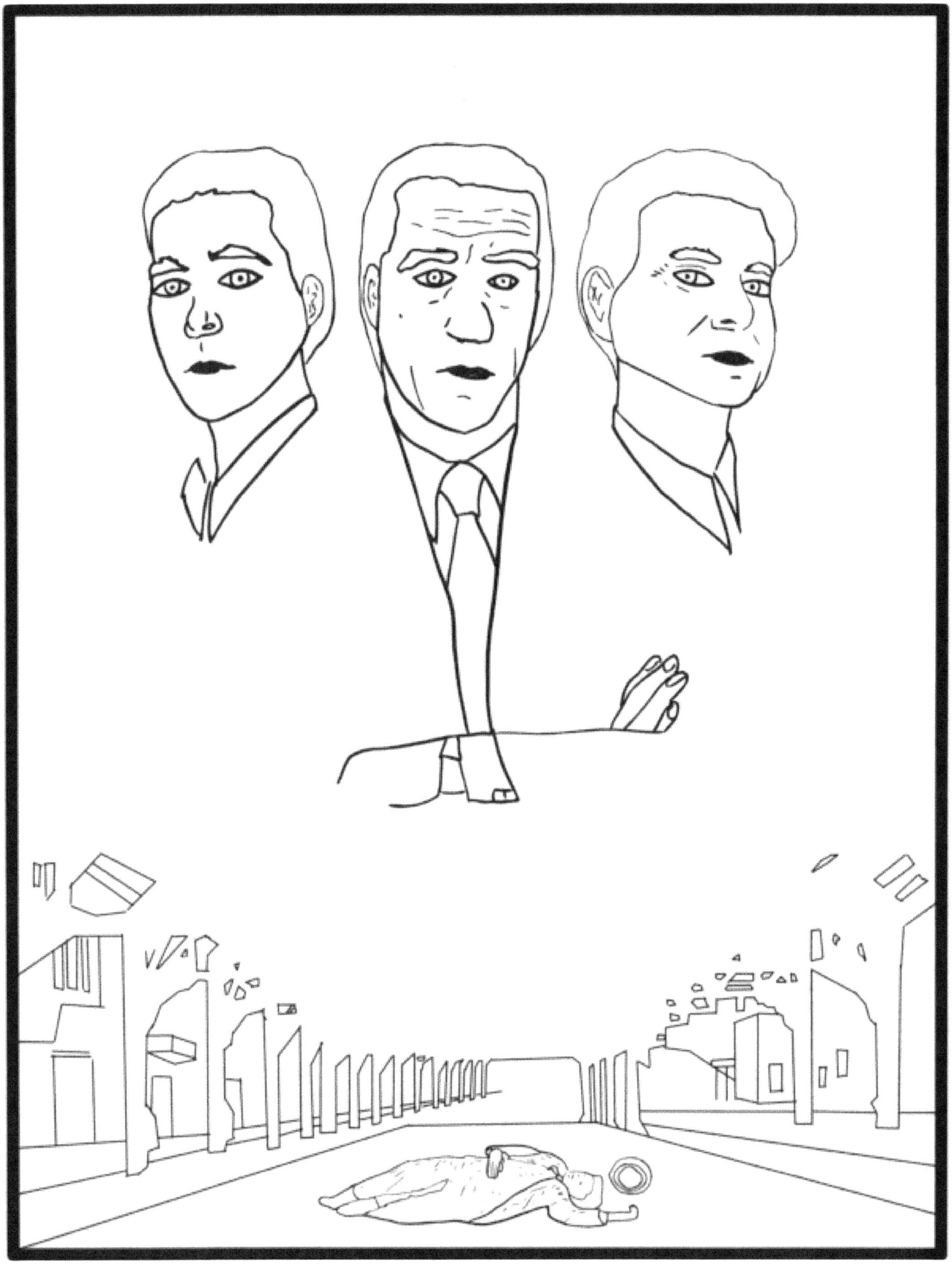

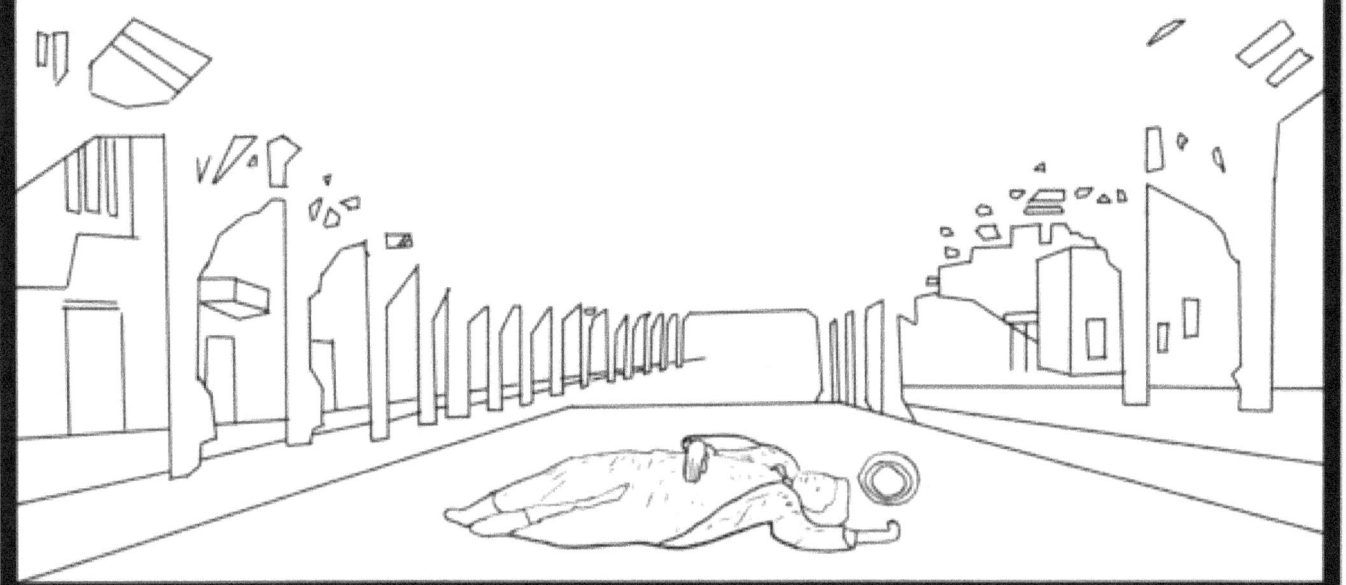

(1990)
GOODFELLAS

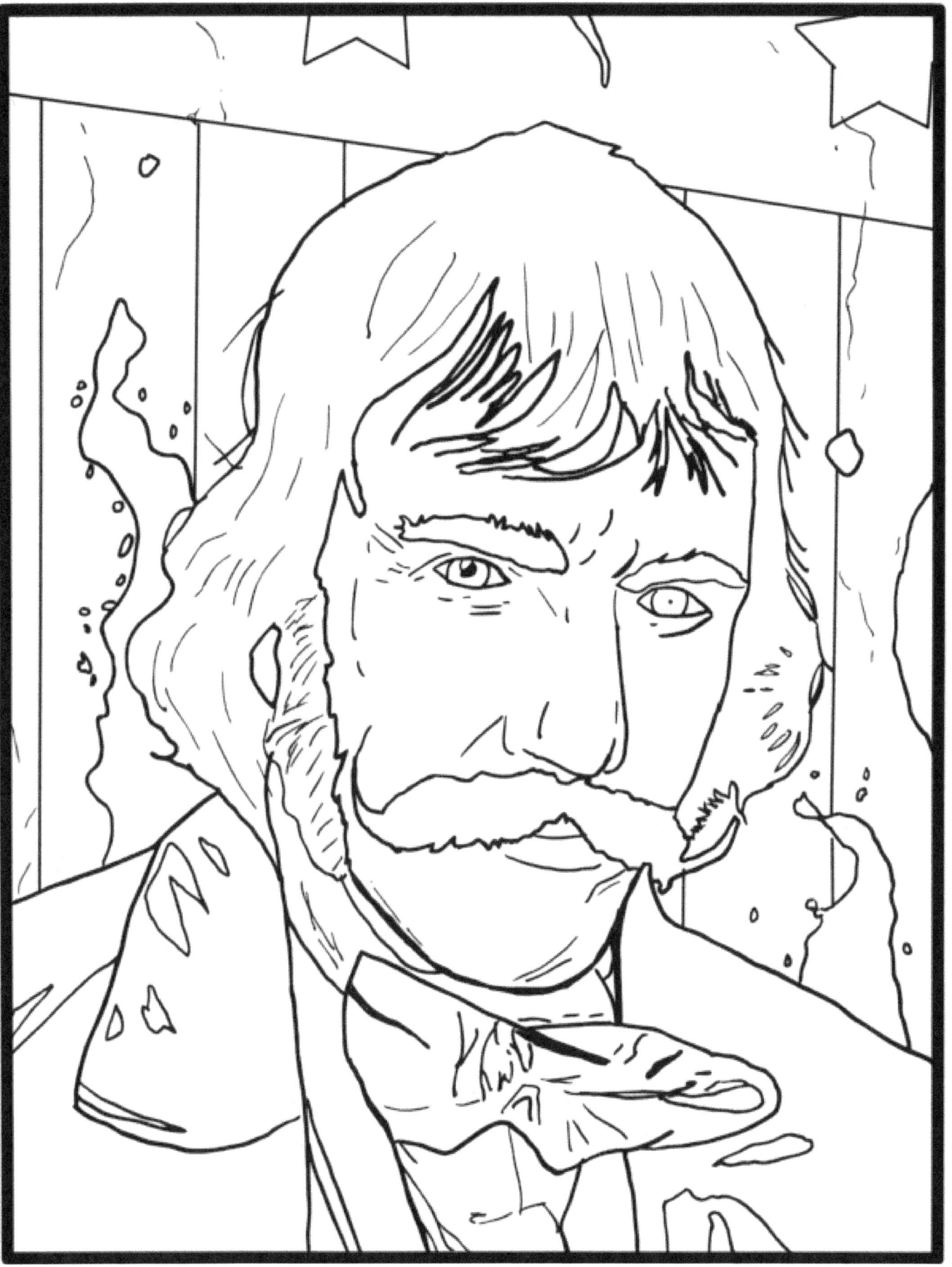

(2002)
GANGS OF NEW YORK

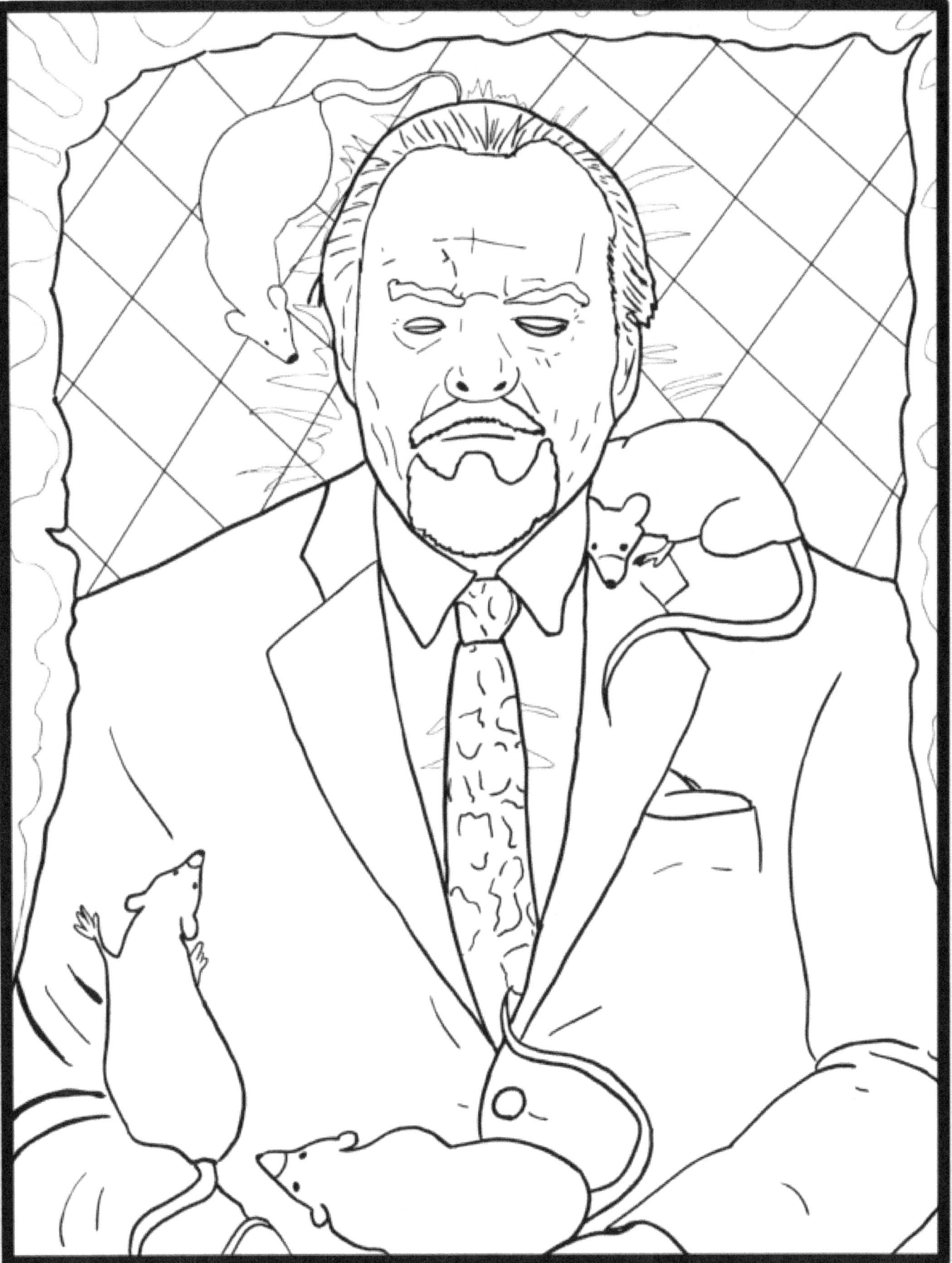

(2006)
THE
DEPARTED

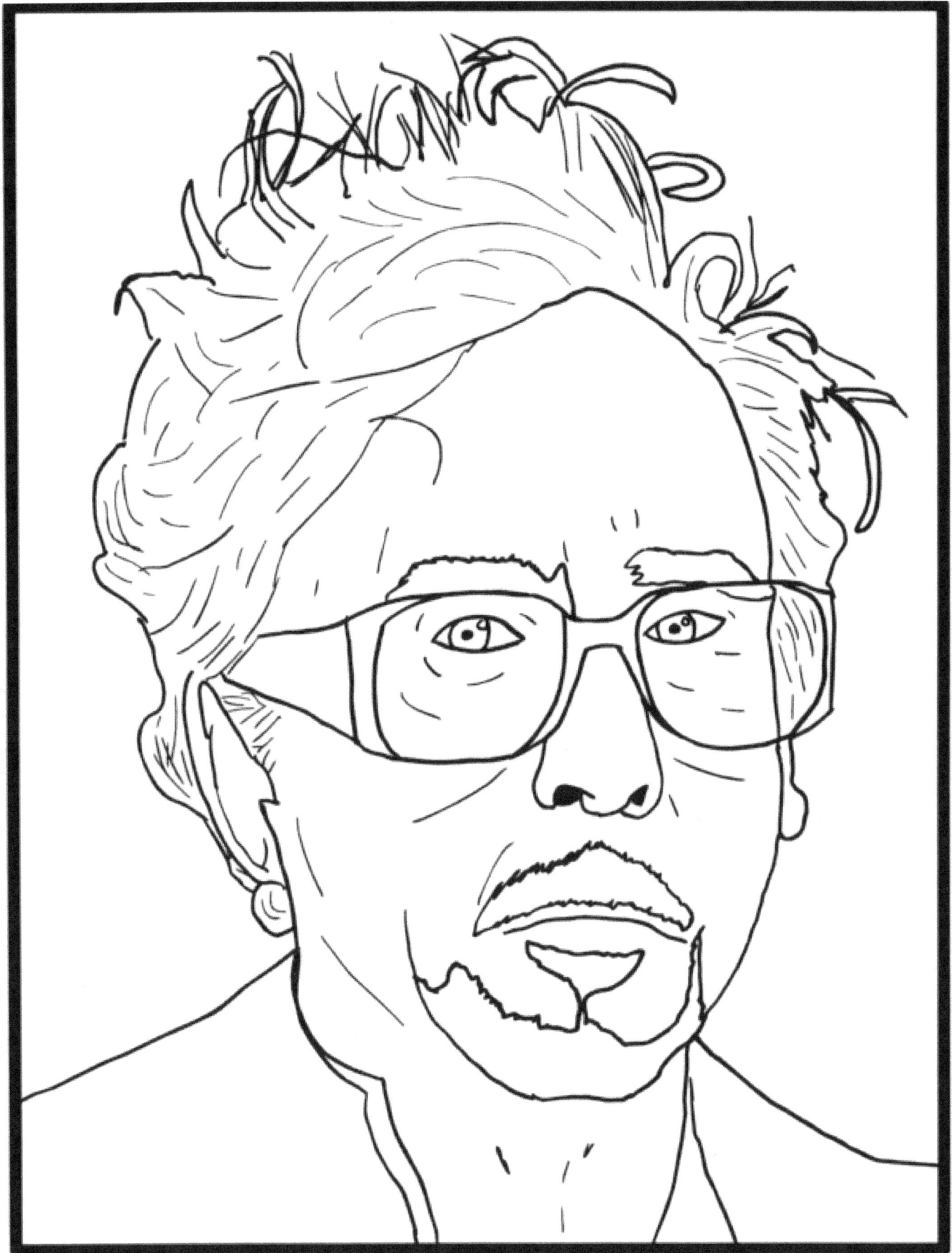

DIRECTOR
TIM BURTON

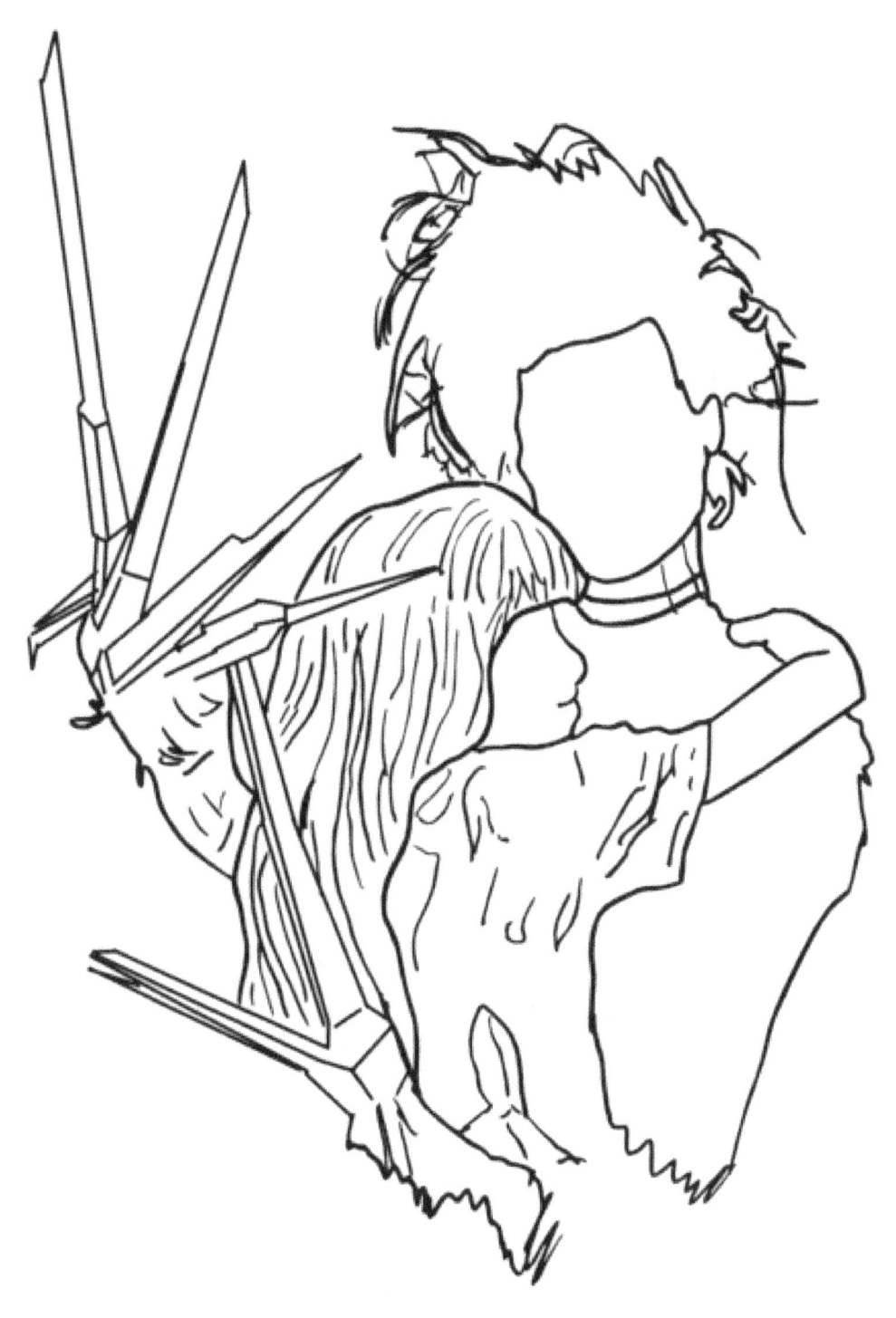

(1990)
EDWARD SCISSORHANDS

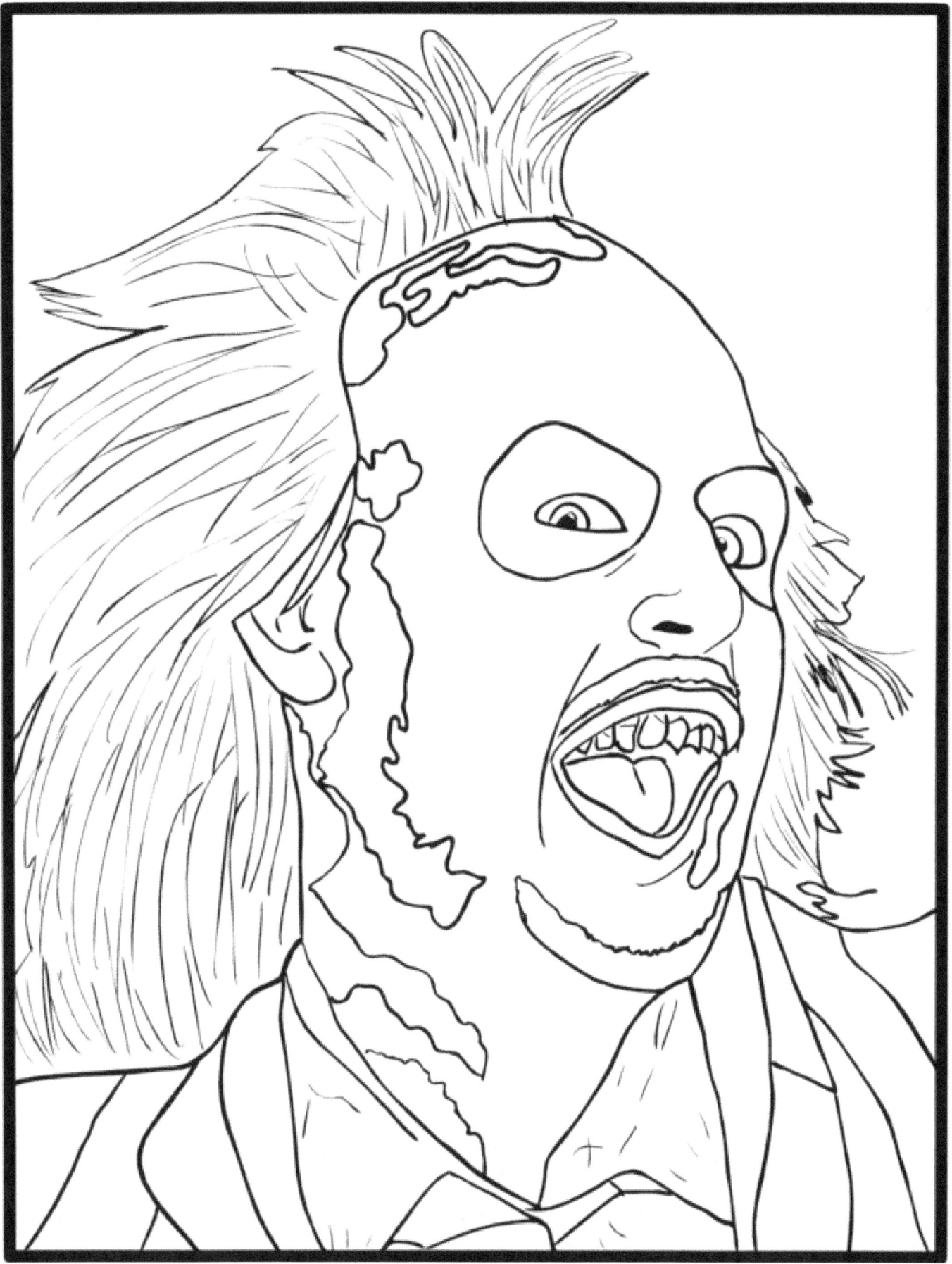

(1988)
Beetlejuice

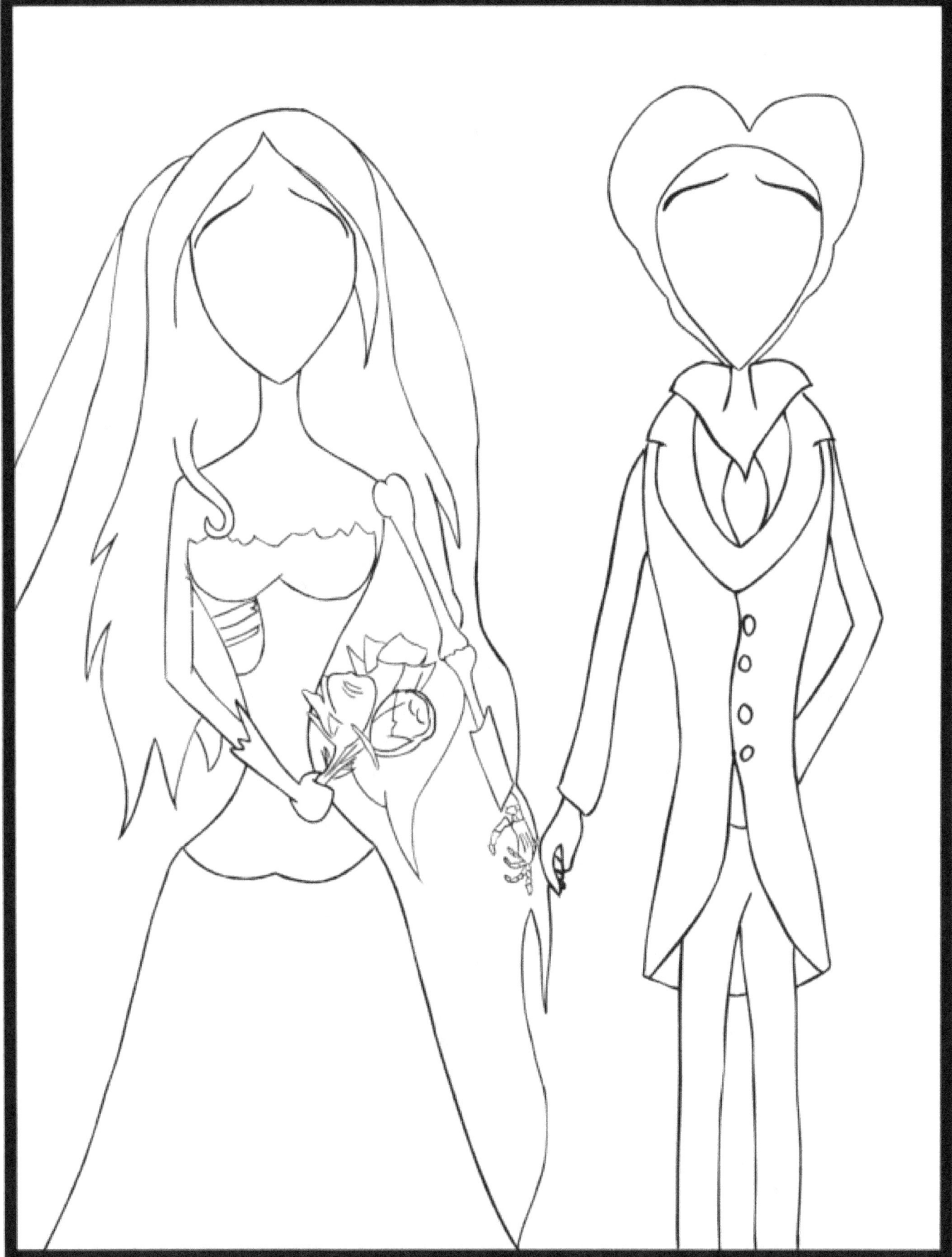

(2005)
CORPSE BRIDE

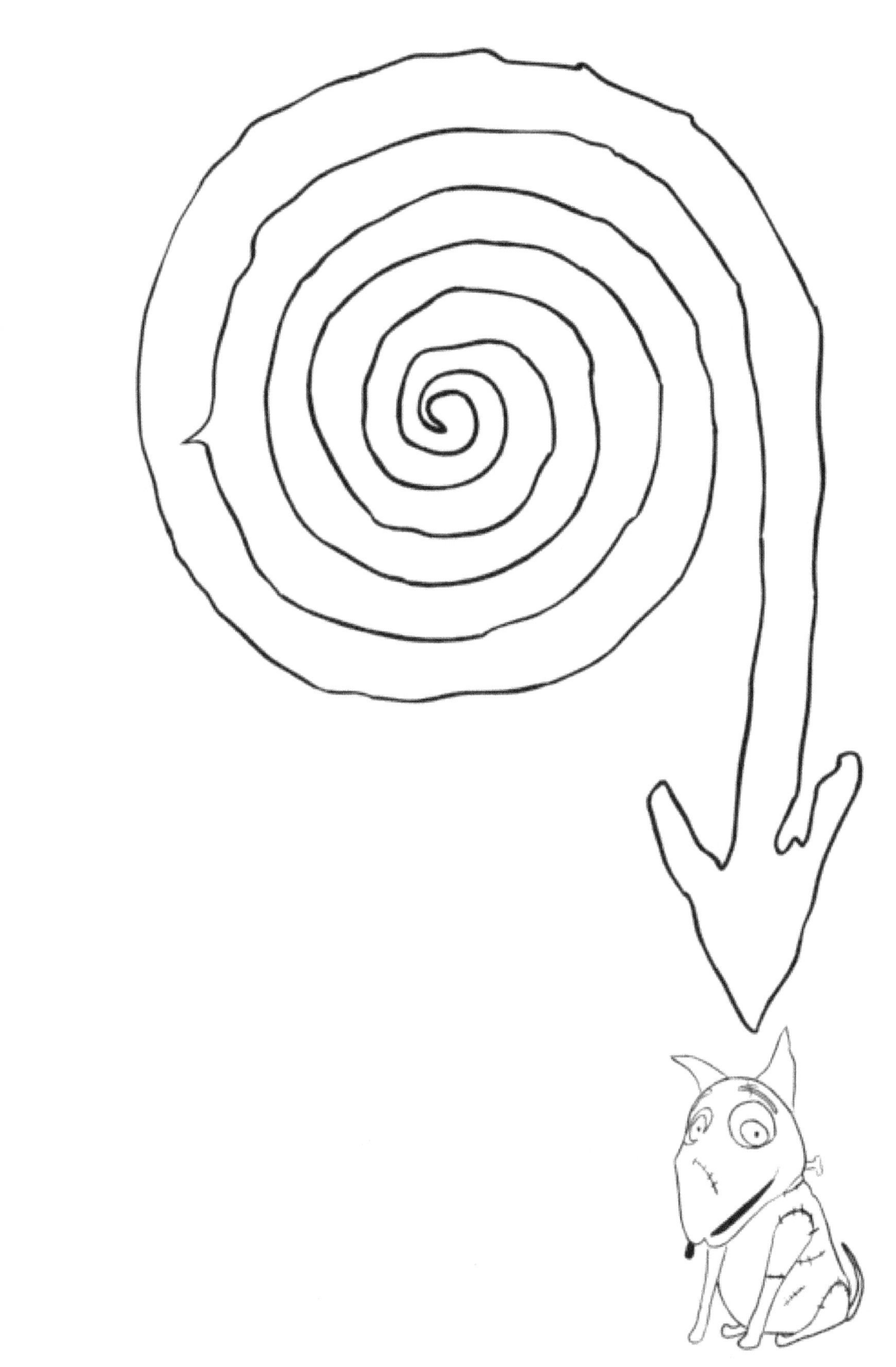

(2012)
FRANKENWEENIE

combined with the TIM BURTON Painting "The Last of its kind"

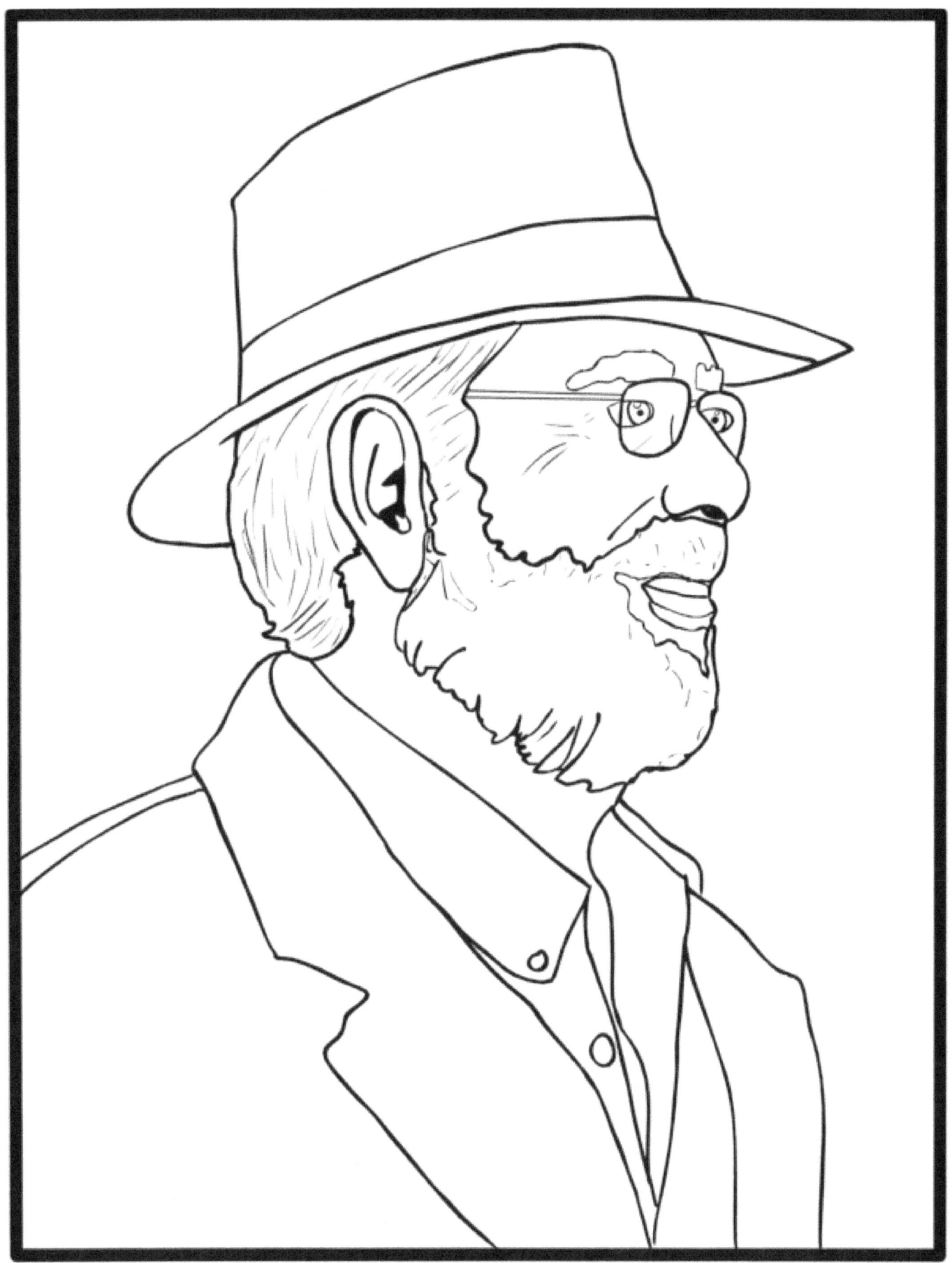

DIRECTOR FRANCIS FORD COPPOLA

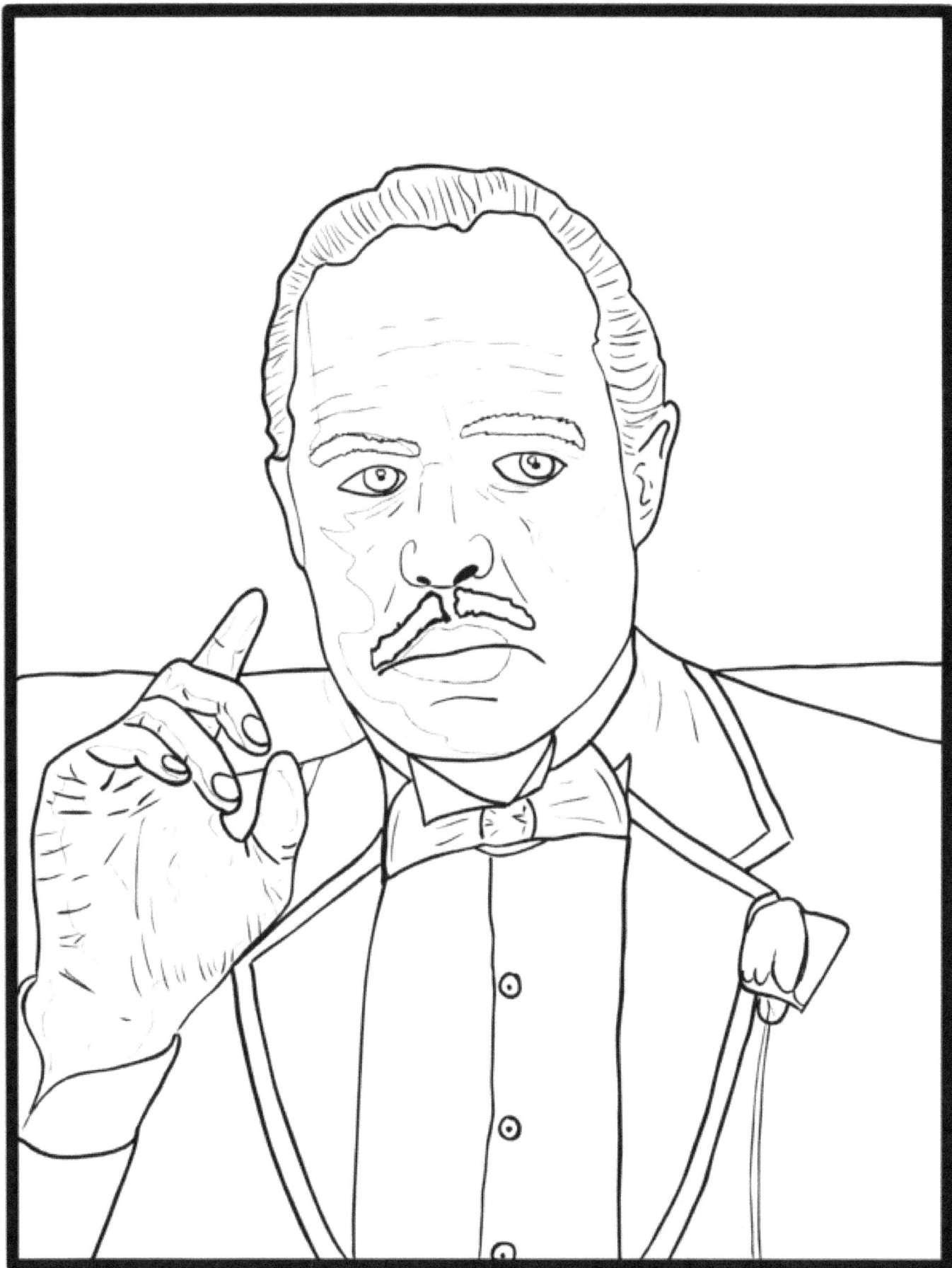

(1972)
THE GODFATHER

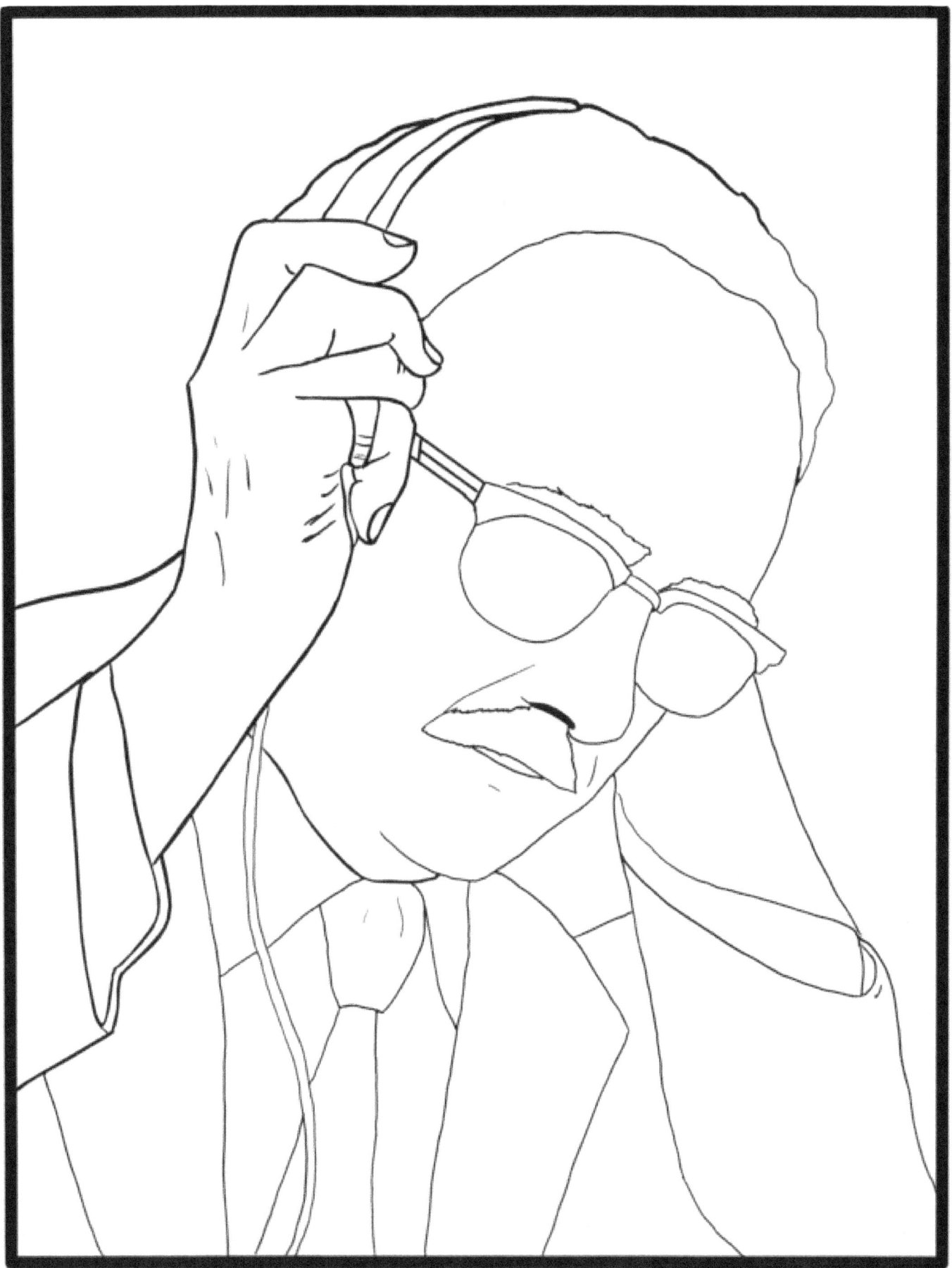

(1974)
THE CONVERSATION

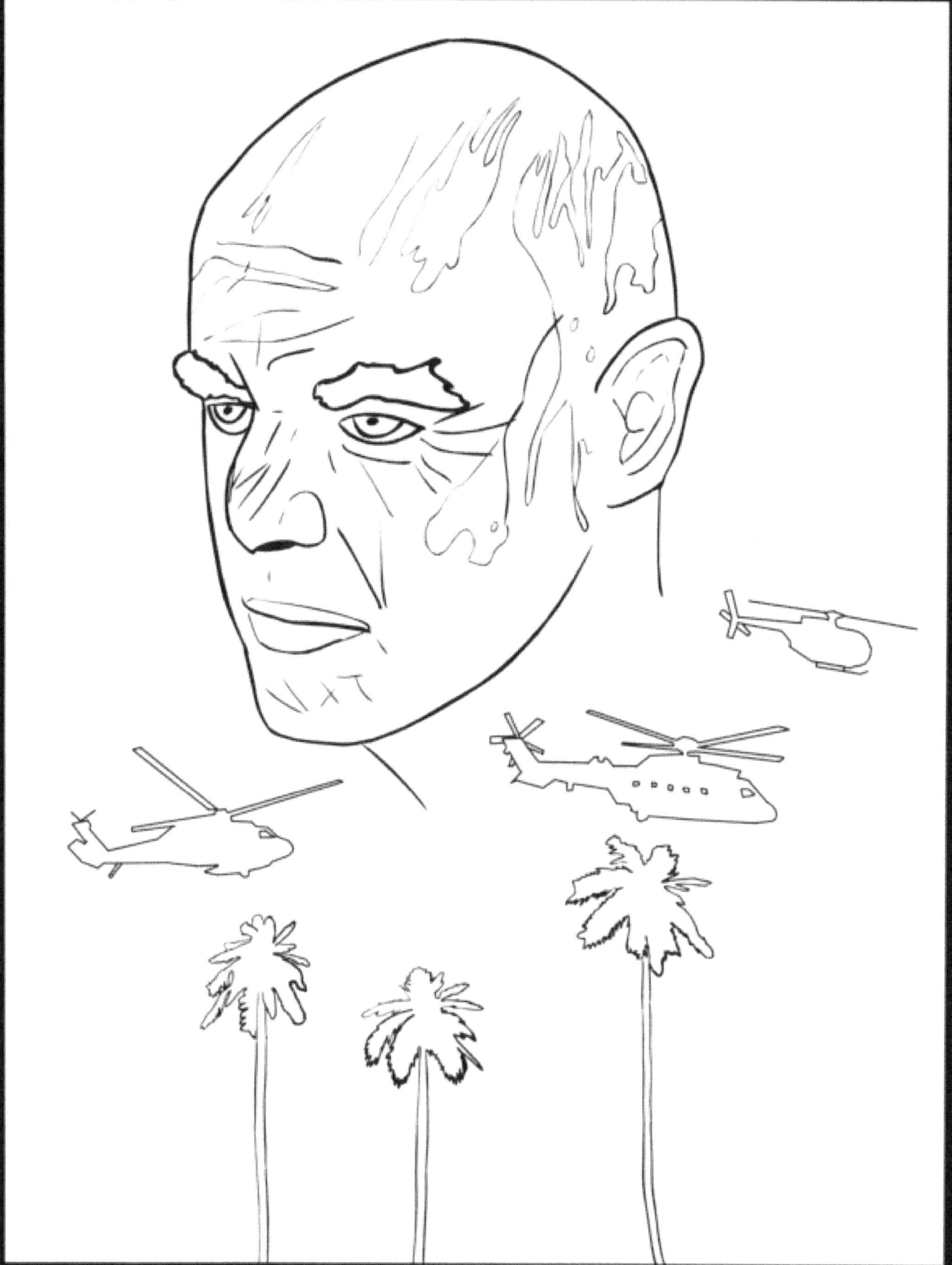

(1979)
APOCALYPSE NOW

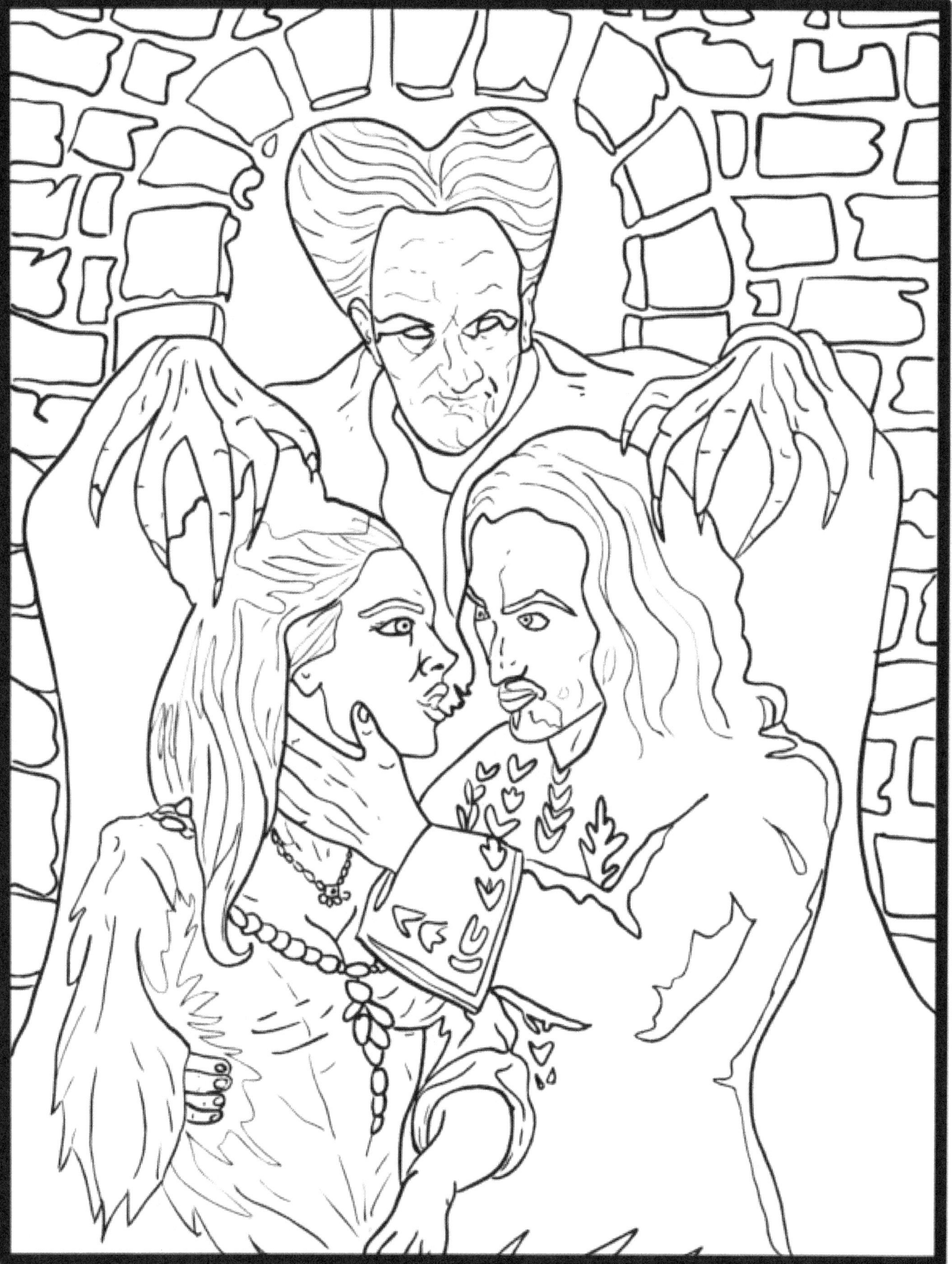

(1992)
BRAM STOKERS DRACULA

www.ingramcontent.com/pod-product-compliance
Lightning Source LLC
Chambersburg PA
CBHW081059240526
45465CB00025B/2767